THE AUTOBIOGRAPHY OF SAINT GEMMA GALGANI

SAINT GEMMA GALGANI

TRANSLATED BY
REVEREND WILLIAM BROWNING C.P.

CATHOLIC WAY
PUBLISHING

ISBN-13: 978-1-78379-268-9

13 12 11 10 9 8 7 6 5 4

Available in E-Book.

www.catholicwaypublishing.com
London, England, UK
2013

CONTENTS

PART V

PART VI

PART VII

PART VIII

TRANSLATOR'S PREFACE

Many years ago, when I was a young priest, I had the good fortune of studying for a time in Rome. During that time, I lived with the Passionist Community at their central house in Rome, Sts. John and Paul. This was an international community of Passionists, but largely Italian, and the language of the house was Italian. As a result, I ended my stay in Rome with at least some knowledge of the Italian language.

I returned to the States with many memories, and with a desire to put my acquired knowledge of Italian to some practical use. Among many other Roman experiences, I had come into more direct contact with the person and the writings of St. Gemma Galgani. Gemma was a young lay woman who desired ardently to become a Passionist Nun, but God never granted this desire. However, through her close association with the Passionists, she earned a treasured place among the Passionist Family. As so many others have done through the years, I found that I had fallen under the spell of St. Gemma. And so, when it came to a way of putting my knowledge of Italian to use, I naturally thought of doing something with the writings of St. Gemma, which, until that time remained locked in the Italian, at least as far as English readers were concerned.

It may be a cause of surprise for many, even now, to learn that this humble and hidden saint wrote a great deal. There are two large volumes of her writings published in Italian. One volume, Lettere di S.Gemma Galgani contains 459 pages of her letters alone. Another, Estasi—Diario—AutobiografiaScritti Vari di S. Gemma Galgani contains 316 pages of her other writings. One does not have to read far in either of these volumes to be completely captivated by the simple and humble saint.

Gemma wrote her autobiography at the insistent request of Father Germanus, C.P., who became her spiritual director in January 1900, approximately three years before her death. At first he directed his spiritual daughter by letter, coming to Lucca to see her for the first time in September 1900. He found Gemma writing a diary of the graces she received day by day. She was writing this diary under obedience to her regular confessor, Msgr. Volpi, Auxiliary Bishop of Lucca. Judging on general principles that it was not good to concentrate to such an extent on what was happening within, Father Germanus ordered her to stop and made her hand over to him all that she had written. But later, as he read the diary, he realized that while the principle on which he had acted was true, it did not apply to Gemma's case. He realized, in short, that he was dealing with a most extraordinary person.

In order to remedy this mistake, he asked her to write for him a general confession of all her sins that he might be better able to direct her. He knew that she could not write of her sins without telling the graces which made them appear so great to her. Gemma complied with his wish, though with great reluctance as is indicated by the autobiography itself.

In her letters, Gemma always refers to this document as her general confession. At the same time, however, it is evident that she did not look upon it as a sacramental confession. At least twice in the pages of the autobiography she passes over points, explaining that she will tell him in confession.

The autobiography thus written in obedience to Father Germanus filled 93 pages of a notebook, all written in her own hand. It covers the years from her infancy until September 1900, when she was 22 years old. She began writing the autobiography on February 17, 1901, and finished it in May of the same year. Since she died two years later on April 11, 1903, it does not cover the last two years of her life.

The manuscript copy of the autobiography still exists and is on display at Sts. John and Paul in Rome. Gemma's beautiful handwriting is still plain, but a remarkable fact about the notebook is that every page has the appearance of having been burned. Father Germanus explains this phenomenon in his life of St. Gemma:

"Gemma's manuscript, when finished, was by my orders given to the charge of her adopted mother, Signora Cecilia Giannini, who kept it hidden in a drawer awaiting the first opportunity of handing it to me. Some days elapsed and Gemma thought she saw the Demon pass through the window of the room where the drawer was, chuckling, and then disappearing in the air. Accustomed as she was to such apparitions, she thought nothing of it. But he, having returned shortly after to molest her, as often happened, with a repulsive temptation, and having failed, left gnashing his teeth and declaring exultantly: 'War, war, your book is in my hands.' So she wrote to tell me. Then, owing to the obedience which she was under to disclose to her vigilant benefactress everything extraordinary that happened to her, she thought she was obliged to tell her what had occurred. They went, opened the drawer, and found that the book was no longer there. I was written to at once and it was easy to imagine my consternation at having lost such a treasure. What was to be done? I thought a great deal about it, and just then, while at the tomb of Blessed Gabriel of the Dolors, a fresh idea came to my mind. I resolved to exorcise the devil and thus force him to return the manuscript if he had really taken it. With my ritual stole and holy water I went to the tomb of the blessed servant of God and there, although nearly four hundred miles from Lucca, I pronounced the exorcism in regular form. God seconded my ministry, and at the same hour the writing was restored to the place from which it had been taken several days before. But in what a state! The pages from top to bottom were all smoked, and parts burned, as if each one had been separately exposed over a strong fire. Yet they were not so badly burned as to destroy the writing. This document, having thus passed through a hell fire, is in my hands."

Having seen the Autobiography as it is preserved today, I can witness personally the evidence described by Father Germanus. We leave it to the reader to judge why the devil was so jealous of this document.

My translation of the Autobiography was published in two places at the time: "The Passionist," July 1954; and "Cross and Crown," June and September 1955. It gives me much pleasure that the Autobiography of St. Gemma is being republished in its present form. One final note, in both of the above publications the name Columban Browning, C.P. was given as the translator. Sometime after that, I returned to my baptismal name.

Rev. William Browning, C.P.

AUTOBIOGRAPHY

To my dear Father, who will burn it immediately. My dear Father, You must understand that at first I intended to make a general confession of my sins without adding anything else, but your Guardian Angel reproved me, and told me to obey and give a short summary of all that has happened in my life both good and bad.

How difficult it is, dear Father, to obey in this matter! But please be careful. You may read and reread this as often as you wish but do not show it to anyone else, and when you are through with it burn it up immediately. Do you understand?

The angel promised to help me recall everything to mind. I told him plainly and pleaded with him that I do not want to do this. I was frightened at the thought of recalling everything, but the Angel assured me that he would help me.

I think, dear Father, that when you read this and learn of all my sins you will be angry with me and will no longer want to be my Father. Still I hope that you will always be willing . . . So prepare yourself to learn of every kind of sin.

And you, dear Father, do you approve of what the angel told me, that I should speak of my whole life? That's his order and I take for granted that's what is in your mind and heart. By writing everything, both good and bad, you will be able to see better how bad I have been and how good others have been to me. You will see how ungrateful I have shown myself toward Jesus and how much I have failed to listen to the good advice of my parents and teachers. So I begin the task, dear Father. Live Jesus!

SAINT GEMMA GALGANI

PART I

EARLIEST MEMORIES—HER MOTHER

The first thing I remember is that when I was a little girl not seven years old, my mother used to take me into her arms and often when she did this she cried and said to me: "I have prayed so much that Jesus would give me a little girl. He has given me this consolation; it is true, but too late. I am ill," she would say to me, "and I must die. I must leave you. Oh, if I could only take you with me! Would you come?" I understood very little of this but I wept because I saw my mother weeping. "And where are you going?" I asked her. "To heaven with Jesus and the angels," she replied. It was my mother, dear Father, who first made me want to go to heaven when I was just a little child. And when I still show this desire, I am reprimanded and receive an emphatic "No" for an answer.[1]

But when my mother asked me this I told her that I did want to go with her. And I remember that when she spoke so often of taking me to heaven with her I did not want to be separated from her. I would not even leave her room.

---

[1] Her confessor, Msgr. Volpi and Father Germanus would not let her pray to die.

The doctor forbade me to go near mother's bed but such a command was useless for I did not obey. Every evening before going to bed I would go to her and, kneeling beside her bed, I would say my prayers. One evening she had me add to the usual prayers a De Profundis to the souls in Purgatory and five Gloria's to the Wounds of Jesus. I said these prayers but as usual carelessly and without attention (all my life I have never paid attention to my prayers). I made a great show over it, complaining to my mother that these were too many prayers to say and I didn't want to say them. And she, indulgent as she was, shortened the prayers after that.

CONFIRMATION, 1885

HER MOTHER IN HEAVEN, 1886

Meanwhile, the time was coming when I was to receive Confirmation. I wanted to take some instructions because I knew nothing. But, bad as I was, I would not leave my mother's room and a Catechist had to come to our house every evening where I took the instructions in the presence of my mother.

On the 26th of May 1885[2] I received Confirmation but I did so weeping. For after the function there was to be a Mass and I was always afraid that Mother would go away (die) without taking me with her.

I assisted at the Mass as best I could, all the while praying for her. All of a sudden I heard a voice in my heart saying to me: "Are you willing to give your mother to me?" "Yes," I answered, "if you will take me, too." "No," replied the voice,

---

[2] In the manuscript of the diary the date is not correct. She does not give the day of the month, and she states that it was the year 1888. The date given here corrects her mistake and is taken from the baptismal register.

"give me your mother willingly. But you must remain with your father for the present. I will take your mother to heaven, understand? Do you give her to me willingly?" I was forced to give my consent. When the Mass was over I ran home. Oh, my God! I looked at Mother and wept. I simply could not contain myself.[3]

Two more months passed. I never left her side. But finally my father, who feared that I would die before Mother, forced me to leave one day and took me to the home of my mother's brother who lived near Lucca. Father, dear Father, such was my lot. What a torture it was! I did not see anyone, neither my father nor my brothers. I learned that my mother died on September 17 of that year.[4]

AT S. GENNARO WITH HER UNCLE

My life was changed when I went to live with my uncle. My aunt was there but she was in no way like my mother. She was good and religious but was interested in the Church only to a certain point. I had formerly complained that my mother had made me pray too much. But all the time that I was with my aunt I could not even go to confession (which I wanted so much). I had been to confession only seven times and I wanted to go every day after the death of my mother (my mother had made me go every week after my confirmation).

My aunt decided to keep me as her daughter but my brother, who is now dead[5], learned of it and would not allow it. So, on Christmas day I returned to my family and lived with my father, my brothers, my two sisters (one of whom I

---

[3] This is the earliest heavenly locution mentioned by Gemma. She was then seven years and two months old.

[4] The year is 1886.

[5] Her brother Gino who died as a cleric in 1894.

did not know because she had been taken away shortly after her birth) and two servants.

What consolation I experienced on returning to my family and being out of the hands of my aunt! She wanted the best for me, but I wanted none of it. My father then sent me to school at the Institute of St. Zita which was conducted by nuns.[6]

During the time when I was with my aunt I was always bad. She had a son who was always tormenting me, pulling my hands behind me. One day when he was on a horse (15 hands high) my aunt told me to take him some kind of a coat to put on. I took it to him and when I was near he pinched me. Then I gave him a hard push, and he fell off and hurt his head. In punishment, my aunt tied my hands behind me for the entire day. Thus mistreated I got very angry and I told him so with strong words. I even threatened to get even, but did not do so.

THE SCHOOL OF ST. ZITA FIRST COMMUNION, 1887

I started to school at the Nun's school and it was heaven for me. I immediately expressed my desire to make my first Communion but they found me so bad and so ignorant that they discouraged me from it. They began, however, to instruct me and to give me much good advice. But I only became worse. Nevertheless, my only desire was to make my first Communion soon and they, knowing how strong was my desire, granted my request before long.

The nuns used to have the children make their first Communion in the month of June. The time had come and

---

[6] These nuns were the Oblates of the Holy Spirit, also called the Sisters of St. Zita. They were founded by the Servant of God, Elena Guerra.

I had to ask my father's permission to enter the convent for a short time. My father, who was indisposed, did not grant me permission. But I knew a very clever way to make him let me do anything, so I used it and got the permission at once. (Every time my father saw me weeping he would grant me whatever I wanted.) I cried, otherwise I would not have received the permission. In the evening he gave it and early the next morning I went into the convent where I remained for fifteen days. During this time I saw none of my family. But how happy I was! What a heaven it was, dear Father! Once inside the convent, I found it to my liking and ran to the chapel to thank Jesus. I begged him fervently to prepare me for Holy Communion. But I had also another desire besides this. When I was a little girl my mother used to show me the crucifix and tell me that Christ died on the cross for men. Later on, my teachers taught me the same thing but I had never understood it. Now I wanted to know all about the life and Passion of Jesus. I told my teacher of this desire and she began, day by day, to explain these things to me, choosing for this a time when the other children were in bed. She did this, I believe, without the Mother Superior knowing of it.

One evening when she was explaining something to me about the crucifixion, the crowning with thorns, and all the sufferings of Jesus, she explained it so very well that a great sorrow and compassion came over me. So much so that I was seized immediately with fever so intense that I was forced to remain in bed all the next day. From that day on the teacher explained such things only briefly.[7]

These nuns caused me some disquiet. They wanted to inform my father that I had contracted the fever. But it did cause a lot of trouble, not only for me but for them and for

---

[7] This nun's name was Sister Camilla Vagliensi.

the whole convent. This happened especially during the ten days of the retreat.[8]

With eleven other children I began the retreat on the[9] day of June. Father Raphael Cianetti preached the retreat. All the children devoted themselves eagerly to prepare well to receive Jesus. Among so many, only I was very negligent and distracted. I gave no thought to changing my life. I listened to the sermons but very soon forgot what I heard.

Often, even every day, that good Father said: "He who eats of Jesus[10] will live of his life." These words filled me with much consolation and I reasoned with myself: Therefore when Jesus comes to me I will no longer live of myself because Jesus will live in me. And I nearly died of the desire to be able to say these words soon (Jesus lives in me). Sometimes I would spend whole nights meditating on these words, being consumed with desire. Finally the day I wanted so much arrived. The day before I wrote these few lines to my father: Dear Papa, Today is the vigil of my first Holy Communion, a day of great joy for me. I write these lines to assure you of my affection and to beg you to pray to Jesus that the first time he comes to me he may find me disposed to receive all those graces that he has prepared for me.

I beg your pardon for all the displeasures and all the disobedience that I have been guilty of, and I beg you this evening to forget all these things. Asking your blessing, I am Your affectionate daughter, GEMMA I prepared myself, with much work on the part of those good nuns, for my general

---

[8] Since she mentioned above that she stayed at the convent fifteen days, we must suppose that she remained there five days after her first Communion. Msgr. Volpi confirms this.

[9] Gemma omits the day and also wrongly states that she made her first Communion in March. There is sufficient evidence that she made her first Communion on Sunday, June 19, 1887.

[10] She actually writes: "He who eats of the life of Jesus . . ."

confession. I made it in three sessions to Msgr. Volpi.[11] I finished it on Saturday, the vigil of that happy day. Finally, Sunday morning came. I arose early and ran to Jesus for the first time. At last my desires were realized. I understood for the first time the promise of Jesus: "He who eats of me shall live of my life."

Dear Father, I do not know how to tell what passed between Jesus and me at that moment. Jesus made himself felt very strongly by my poor soul. I understood at that moment that the delights of heaven are not like those of the earth. I felt myself overcome by the desire to render that union with my God continual. I felt weary of the world more and more, and more disposed to recollection. It was that same morning that Jesus gave me the great desire to be a religious.

FIRST COMMUNION RESOLUTIONS

Before leaving the convent I made certain resolutions regarding the conduct of my life:

§ 1. I will receive Confession and Communion each time as though it were my last.

§ 2. I will visit Jesus in the Blessed Sacrament often, especially when I am afflicted.

§ 3. I will prepare myself for every feast of our Blessed Mother by some mortification, and every evening I will ask my heavenly Mother's blessing.

§ 4. I want to remain always in the presence of God.

---

[11] Msgr. Giovanni Volpi, who was made bishop in 1897. He was Gemma's ordinary confessor until her death.

§ 5. Every time the clock strikes I will repeat three times: My Jesus, mercy. I would have liked to add other resolutions to these but my teacher would not permit it. And she had good reason, for within a year after I returned to my family I had forgotten these resolutions as well as the good advice I had received and I became worse than before. I continued to go to school to the nuns and they were fairly satisfied with me. I went to Communion two or three times a week and Jesus made himself felt ever stronger. Several times he made me feel very great consolation. But as soon as I left him, I began to be proud, more disobedient than before, a bad example to my companions and a scandal to all.

At school, not a day passed on which I was not punished. I did not know my lessons and I was almost expelled. At home I would not let anyone have peace. Every day I wanted to go for a walk, always wearing new clothes which my poor father provided me for a long time. I ceased to say my usual prayers morning and evening. But while I was committing all these sins I never forgot to recite every day three Hail Mary's with my hands under my knees (a practice my mother had taught me that Jesus might protect me every day from sins against holy purity).[12]

---

[12] In her writings, Gemma frequently speaks of her sins in superlatives. Her horror for what she called her sins indicates how greatly she was enlightened by God.

PART II

CHARITY TOWARD THE POOR NEW CONVERSION

During this time which lasted almost an entire year, the only thing I had left was charity to the poor. Every time I left the house I asked my father for money. If he sometimes refused it, I would take bread, flour, or some such thing. And God himself would see to it that I met some poor people, for every time I left the house there would be three or four. To those who came to the door I would give clothes or whatever else I had.

But then my confessor forbade me to do these things and I stopped doing them. In this way Jesus worked in me a new conversion. For my father no longer gave me money, I could take nothing from the house, and every time I went out I met none but poor people and they all ran after me. I could not give them anything. This pained me so that I wept continually. For this reason I quit going out except when I really had to. The result was that I grew tired of clothes and everything else.

I wanted to make another general confession but I was not permitted to do so.[13] I did confess everything however,

---

[13] These words are a confirmation of the innocence of Gemma. Her confessor knew her well and prudently judged that she did not need a general confession.

and Jesus gave me such a deep sorrow for my sins that I felt it always. I asked pardon of my teachers because I had displeased them most of all. But this change did not please my father and my brothers. One brother especially chided me because I wanted to go to Mass every morning. But from then on Jesus helped me more than ever.

LIVING WITH HER AUNTS

At this time, as my grandfather and uncle were dead, two of my aunts, my father's sisters, came to live with us.[14] They were good, religious and affectionate, but their affection was never the tender love of a mother. They took us to church every day and they were diligent in instructing us in the religion.

Among us brothers and sisters some were better and some worse. The oldest boy, the fourth of our family to die, and the youngest girl, Julia, were the best, and so were more loved by my aunts. But the others, who took my bad example, were far more lively and so less appreciated. Nonetheless, none of us lacked what was needed.

I was always the worst of all and who knows what a strict account I must give to the Lord for the bad example that I gave to my brothers and companions!! My aunts never failed to correct me in all my failings but I responded arrogantly, giving them many short answers.

Now, as I have said, Jesus used my prohibition to give alms as means to convert me. I began to think of how much my sins offended Jesus. I began also to study and work harder, and my teachers continued to encourage me. The one defect for which I was often reproved and punished was my pride. My teacher frequently called me "pride personified."

---

[14] The two nuns were Elisa and Elna Galgani.

Yes, this was my greatest sin but only Jesus knows whether I realized it or not. Many a time I fell on my knees before my teacher and all the class, and even the Mother Superior, to beg pardon for this sin. And also many a time in the evening I wept when I was alone. I was not aware of this sin and every day I fell into it time and again without adverting to it.

A GOOD TEACHER

The teacher who at the time of my retreat had explained the Passion to me reproved me one day and explained the matter to me (perhaps because she had noticed a change in me). But she did so little by little. She often said to me: "Gemma, you belong to Jesus and you should be all his. Be good. Jesus is pleased with you and you need much help. Meditation on the Passion ought to be something very close to your heart. Oh, if you could always be with me."

That good teacher had detected my desire. At other times she said to me: "Gemma, what graces Jesus has given you!" I, who never understood all this, remained as one dumb. But sometimes I felt the need of a little talk and (I don't hesitate to say it) of a caress from my dear teacher so I ran looking for her. Sometimes she would appear very serious and when I saw her like that I would cry. Then she would take me into her arms (even though I was eleven years old) and caress me. As a result I was so attached to her that I called her my mother.

RETREAT OF 1891

Every two years the nuns used to have a retreat which was open also to the external students. It hardly seemed true that I could commune so intimately with Jesus again. But this time I was all alone without any help, for the nuns were making their own retreat at the same time as the children. I understood well that Jesus was giving me this opportunity to know myself better and to purify myself and please him more. The retreat was held in 1891 and during this time Gemma was to be completely changed as to give herself entirely to Jesus. I recall the words which that good priest repeated so often: "Let us remember that we are nothing and that God is all. God is our creator and all that we have he has given us." I remember that after a few days of the retreat the preacher had us make a meditation on sin. It was then that I came to realize, dear Father, that I was worthy only to be despised by all. I saw myself to be so ungrateful to God, guilty as I was of so many sins.

Then we made a meditation on hell, of which I knew myself to be deserving, and during this meditation I made this resolution: I will make acts of contrition during the day, especially when I have committed some fault. During the last days of the retreat we considered the example of humility, meekness, obedience and patience (of Jesus). And from this meditation I formed two more resolutions:

§ 1. To make a visit to Jesus in the Blessed Sacrament every day and speak to him more with the heart than with the tongue.

§ 2. I will try harder to avoid speaking of indifferent things and to speak rather of heavenly things. At the end of the retreat I obtained permission from my confessor to receive communion three times a week and likewise to go to confession three times a week, and I continued to do this for three or four years, until 1895.

MEDITATION ON THE PASSION OF JESUS

I continued to go to school every day but the desire to receive Jesus and to know more about his Passion increased, so much so that I succeeded in getting my teacher to explain it to me for an entire hour after every ten hours of work or study. I desired nothing else. Every day I worked or studied ten hours and spent an hour listening to the explanation of some point on the Passion. Many times as I thought of my sins and my ingratitude to Jesus, we began to weep together.

It was during these four years that this good teacher taught me also to perform some little penance for Jesus. The first was the wearing of a little rope around my body, and there were many others. But no matter how hard I tried, I never obtained the permission of my confessor for these things. Therefore she taught me rather to mortify my eyes and my tongue. She succeeded in making me better but with much difficulty.

This good teacher died after having led me along for six years.[15] Then I came under the direction of another who was fully as good as the first.[16] But she also had to reprove me often for the ugly sin of pride.

Under her direction I began to have a great desire to pray more. Every evening as soon as school was out I would go home and shut myself up in my room and recite the entire rosary on my knees. And often I would rise during the night for about a quarter of an hour to recommend my poor soul to Jesus.

---

[15] This is an error on Gemma's part, either of memory or writing. Sister Camilla died in March 1888. Gemma, who entered the Institute in 1887, could have had her as a teacher for only one year.
[16] This new teacher was Giulia Sestini.

PART III

HER FATHER'S BENJAMIN HER BROTHER GINO

My aunts and my brothers did not pay such attention to me. They let me do whatever I wanted because they knew how bad I was. But my father always took great delight in me. He often said (and this often made me cry): "I have only two children, Gino and Gemma." He said such things in the presence of all the others, and to tell the truth we were about the most mischievous in the house. I loved Gino more than the rest. We were always together. During vacation time we would amuse ourselves by making little altars, celebrating feats etc., and in this we were always alone. As he grew up he had the desire of becoming a priest. So he was sent to seminary and put on clerical dress, but a few years later he died.[17]

During the time when he was sick in bed he wanted me always near him. The doctor gave up all hope for him. Since I was so sorry that he was going to die, I started using all his things so that I would die too. As a matter of fact, I almost did die. I became very seriously ill about a month later.

I cannot describe the care all lavished on me, especially my father. Many times I saw him weeping and begging Jesus

---

[17] He died on September 11, 1894.

to let him die in my place. He used every means possible to cure me, and after three months I was well again.

SHE LEAVES SCHOOL NECKLACES OF
A SPOUSE OF THE CRUCIFIED

The doctor forbade me to study anymore and I quit school. Many times the superior and the nuns sent for me to come and be with them but my father would not let me go. Every day he took me outside. He gave me everything I wanted. And I began to pamper myself once more. But I kept going to communion three or four times a week and even though I was so bad, Jesus came and dwelt with me and said many things to me.

I recall very well one time I was given a gold watch and chain. Ambitious as I was I could hardly wait to put it on and go out (an indication, dear Father, that my imagination was working on me). I did, in fact, go out with it on and when I returned and started to take it off I saw an angel (whom I recognized immediately as my Guardian Angel) who said to me very seriously: "Remember that the precious jewelry that adorns a spouse of the crucified King can only be thorns and the cross."

I did not even tell my confessor about this. In fact, I now tell it for the first time. These words made me fear as did the angel himself. But a little later, while reflecting on them without understanding them at all, I made this resolution: I resolve for the love of Jesus and to please him, never to wear the watch again and not even to speak of things that savor vanity. At the time I also had a ring on my finger. I took it off immediately and from that day to this I have not worn such things. So I resolved (because Jesus had given me clear lights to the effect that I should be a religious) to change my life. I had a good occasion to do this, for we were about to begin the year of 1896. I wrote in a little notebook: "During this new year I resolve to begin a new life. I do not know what will happen to me during this year. But I abandon myself entirely to you, my God. And my aspirations[18] and all my affections will be for you. I feel so weak, dear Jesus, but with your help I hope and resolve to live a different life, that is, a life closer to you."

DESIRE FOR HEAVEN

From the moment when my mother inspired me with the desire for heaven I have always (even in the midst of so many sins) wanted it ardently. If God had left the choice to me I would have preferred to escape from the body and fly to heaven. Every time a fever came upon me and I felt ill I experienced a great consolation. But this changed to sorrow when, after some illness, I would feel my strength return. One day after Holy Communion I asked Jesus why he did not take me to heaven. He answered: "My daughter, I do not take you because during your life I will give you many occasions to gain more merit, increasing your desire for heaven as you bear the trials of life with patience." These words in no way diminished my desire. Rather I felt it increasing in me day by day.

LOVING JESUS AND SUFFERING WITH HIM

During this same year of 1896 another desire began to grow in me. I began to feel an ever greater yearning to love Jesus Crucified very much, and at the same time a desire to suffer with him and to help him in his sufferings.

---

[18] The word Gemma uses is "inspirations."

One day as I was looking at the crucifix so great a sorrow came over me that I fell to the floor. My father was in the house at the time and he began to reprove me, saying that it was not good for me to stay at home and that I should go out early the next morning (he had not let me go to Mass the last two mornings). I answered in a disturbed tone of voice: "It is not good for me to remain away from Jesus in the Blessed Sacrament." My answer disturbed him because he noticed that my voice was not very strong. I hid myself in a room and there for the first time I gave vent to my sorrow with Jesus alone.

Dear Father, I do not remember the words I spoke, but my angel is here and he tells me what I said word for word. It is as follows: "I want to follow you no matter what the cost in pain, and to follow you fervently. No, Jesus, I do not want to continue displeasing you by a tepid life as I have done up to now. That would amount to coming to you to bring you displeasure. Therefore I resolve to make my prayer more devout and my communions more frequent. Jesus, I want to suffer and to suffer much for you. Prayer will ever be on my lips. If even he falls often who makes frequent resolutions, what will happen to him who resolves but rarely." Dear Father, these words came from my heart in that moment of sorrow and of hope when I was alone with my Jesus. I have made so many resolutions and I never kept any of them. Every day, amid so many sins of every kind, I would ask Jesus to let me suffer and suffer much.

PAIN IN HER FOOT

After a little Jesus sent me a consolation: he sent me a pain in one of my feet. I kept this secret for a while but the pain was severe. A doctor came and said an operation was necessary and perhaps the foot would have to be amputated. All of my family was greatly worried and only I was indifferent. I remember that while they were performing the operation I cried and complained loudly. But then, looking at Jesus, I begged him to pardon my folly. Jesus also sent me other pains and I can say with truth that ever since the death of my mother I have never spent a day without suffering some little thing for Jesus.

During this time I never ceased to commit sins. I became worse every day. I was full of every kind of fault and I do not understand why Jesus never showed himself angry with me. Only once did I see Jesus angry at me and I would rather suffer the pains of hell a thousand times in this life than find myself before Jesus so displeased and to see before my eyes the horrible picture of my soul as I did on the occasion of which I will speak later.[19]

---

[19] See the section under the heading: A Severe Reproof From Jesus.

PART IV

HER FIRST VOW

On Christmas day of 1896 I was permitted to go to Mass and receive Holy Communion. I was about fifteen years old[20] at the time and I had already often asked my confessor for permission to make a vow of virginity (I had asked for this for many years but I did not really know what it was; it only seemed to me that it was the most beautiful adornment I could offer to Jesus). He would not let me take this vow of virginity but instead allowed me to make a vow of chastity. So on Christmas night I made my first vow to Jesus. I remember that Jesus was so pleased with it that he asked me after Holy Communion to unite with this vow the offering of my whole self and all my sentiments in abandonment to his holy will. I did this with such a joy that I spent that night and the next day as if in heaven.

A YEAR OF GREAT SORROW (1897): DEATH OF HER FATHER

That year came to an end and we entered upon the year of 1897 which was a year of great sorrow for all my family. I alone being heartless, remained unmoved in the face of so

---

[20] Actually Gemma was 19 years old. She was born on March 12, 1878. 21. Her father died on November 11, 1897, at the age of 53.

many afflictions. The thing that troubled the others the most was the fact that we were deprived of all means of livelihood, and added to this my father was seriously ill. One morning after communion I understood what a great sacrifice Jesus would ask of us soon. I wept very much but Jesus made himself felt in my soul all the more during those sorrowful days. I saw my father so perfectly resigned to die that I felt strong enough to bear these sorrows very calmly. On the day of his death[21] Jesus told me not to give way to useless weeping and wailing, so I spent the day praying in resignation to the will of God who at that moment took the role of both my heavenly and earthly father.

WITH HER AUNT IN CAMAIORE RETURN TO LUCCA (1898)

After my father's death we found ourselves destitute. We had only enough to live on. One of my aunts, realizing this, helped us a great deal. She was unwilling that I should remain with my family. So the day after my father's death she sent for me and had me stay with her for several months. (This was not the aunt with whom I lived after my mother's death, but another one.)[22]

Every morning she took me to Mass but I seldom received communion because I could not bring myself to go to confession to anyone besides Monsignor. During that time I gradually forgot Jesus once more. I neglected prayer and I began anew to seek diversions.

Another niece of my aunt who was also living with her became very friendly with me and we became very much alike in our wickedness. My aunt sent the two of us out together frequently. And I am sure that if Jesus had not had

---

[21] Her father died on November 11, 1897, at the age of 53.
[22] This aunt was Carolina Galgani, wife of Domenico Lencione.

pity on my weakness I would have fallen into serious sins. Love of the world began gradually to awaken in my soul. But Jesus once more came to the rescue. All of a sudden I became stooped and began to have terrible pains in my back. I bore this for a time but as I saw myself growing worse I asked my aunt to take me back to Lucca. She lost no time, but sent someone back with me.

But, dear Father, the thought of those months spent in sin filled me with terror. I had committed sins of every kind. Even impure thoughts had run through my mind. I had listened to bad conversation instead of fleeing from it. I had told untruths to my aunt to protect my companion. In short, I had stood on the brink of hell.[23]

SERIOUS ILLNESS (1898—1899)

Once again at Lucca, I was better for some time. I never wanted to obey when they wished a doctor to visit me (for I never wanted anyone to touch me or see me.) One evening a doctor came unannounced, examined me by force and found an abscess on my body which he feared was very serious because he thought it had affected my spine.

For a long time I had felt pain in that part of my body but I did not want to touch or look at it because when I was a little girl I had heard a priest say: "Our body is the temple of the Holy Spirit." Those words had struck me and led me to guard my body as closely as possible.

After he had visited me the doctor called a consultant. What affliction it caused me, dear Father, to have to uncover myself. Every time the doctor touched me I cried. After the

---

[23] Here again, Gemma exaggerates her condition. Those who testified as to her condition at the time give an entirely different picture of her.

consultation I grew steadily worse and I was forced to go to bed and was not able to move. Every remedy was used on me but instead of helping me they made me worse. While I was in bed I was ill at ease and a source of annoyance to all.

The second day I was in bed I was not at peace and I wrote to Monsignor telling him that I wanted to see him. He came at once and I made a general confession, not indeed because I was so bad off but to regain peace of conscience which I had lost. After confession my peace with Jesus returned and as a sign of this, on that same evening I experienced a very deep sorrow for my sins.

Then, dear Father, the pain became worse and worse and the doctors decided to operate on me (in that part of which I have spoken). Three doctors came (and what I suffered from the pain was as nothing). I felt pain and suffering only when I found myself in their presence almost entirely unclothed. Dear Father, how much better it would have been for me to die! Finally the doctors saw that all remedies were useless and they gave me up entirely. After that they came to see me only now and then through courtesy, so to speak.

Regarding the nature of this illness, nearly all the doctors said it was a spinal disease and only one insisted that it was hysteria. I had to lie in one position in bed and it was impossible for me to move myself. In order to have a little relief now and then I had to ask some of the family to help me to move an arm, now a leg. They took excellent care of me, but I, on the contrary, repaid them only with bad manners and short answers.[24]

---

[24] Those who attended her took a different view. They portray her as always most patient.

RECEIVES COMFORT FROM HER GUARDIAN ANGEL

One evening when I was more uncomfortable than usual I was complaining to Jesus telling him that I would not have prayed so much if I had known he was not going to cure me, and I asked him why he wanted me to be sick this way. My angel answered me as follows: "If Jesus afflicts you in body it is always in order to purify your soul. Be good." Oh, how many times during my long illness did I not experience consoling words in my heart! But I never profited by them.

The thing that afflicted me most was to have to stay in bed, because I wanted to do what the others were doing. I wanted to go to confession every day and to Mass each morning. But one morning when they brought Holy Communion to me at home Jesus made Himself felt rather strongly in my soul and he gave me a severe rebuke, telling me that I was a weak soul. "It is your bad self—love that makes you resent not being able to do what the others do," he said to me, "and that causes you so much confusion at seeing that you have to be helped by others. If you were dead to yourself you would not be so disturbed."

PART V

ST. GABRIEL OF THE SORROWFUL VIRGIN

During this time my family was making triduums and novenas and having others make them for my cure. But they obtained nothing. I myself remained indifferent. The words of Jesus had strengthened but not converted me.

One day a lady who often came to visit me brought me a book to read (the life of Venerable Gabriel).[25] I took it almost disdainfully and put it on the pillow. The lady begged me to recommend myself to Gabriel but I thought little of it. My family, however, began to say three Paters, Aves, and Gloria's in his honor every day.

One day I was alone. It was a little after noon. I was attacked by a strong temptation and I said within myself that I was tired of all this and staying in bed annoyed me. The devil took advantage of these thoughts and began to tempt me saying that if I had listened to him he would have cured me and would have done all that I asked of him. Dear Father, I was on the point of giving in. I was disturbed and felt that I was conquered. But suddenly a thought came to me. My

---

[25] St. Gabriel of the Sorrowful Virgin, Passionist. At that time he was Venerable.

mind turned to Venerable Gabriel and I said fervently: "The soul comes first and then the body!"

Nevertheless the devil continued with even stronger assaults. A thousand ugly thoughts rushed through my mind. Again I turned to Venerable Gabriel and with his help I conquered. Entering within myself, I made the sign of the Cross and in a quarter of an hour I turned to unite myself with God, whom I so little appreciated. I recall that on that very evening I began to read the life of Brother Gabriel. I read it several times. I never grew tired of reading it and admiring his virtues and his example. My resolutions were many, my deeds but few.

From the day on which my new protector, Venerable Gabriel, saved my soul I began to practice a special devotion to him. At night I could not sleep unless I had his picture under my pillow. And from that day to this I began to see him near me (here, dear Father, I do not know how to express myself; I have felt his presence). In every act, in every bad action that I have performed I thought of Brother Gabriel and thereupon ceased the action. I have never failed to pray to him every day in these words: "The soul comes before the body."

One day the lady who had brought me the life of Venerable Gabriel came to take it back. In taking it from under my pillow and giving it back to her I could not help weeping. The lady, seeing that it was so hard for me to give it up, promised to come back later and get it when the person who had given it to her requested it. She came back a few days later and I had to give it back to her, though I did so weeping. This caused me much displeasure.

But that Saint of God very soon rewarded this little sacrifice for that night in a dream he appeared to me clothed in white. I did not recognize him, dear Father. When he saw that I did not recognize him he opened the white garment and I saw him clothed as a Passionist. I knew him immediately. I remained in silence before him. He asked me why I had cried when they took his life from me. I don't recall what I answered but he said: "See how much your sacrifice has pleased me. It has pleased me so much that I have come myself to see you. Do you wish me well?" I did not answer. Then he comforted me and said to me: "Be good because I will return to see you." He told me to kiss his habit and rosary and then he went away. My imagination started working and I found myself always awaiting another visit from him. But he did not come again for many, many months. Here is how it happened. The feast of the Immaculate Conception came. At that time the Barbantine nuns, Sisters of Charity, were coming to change my clothing and tend to me. Among those who came there was one who was not yet vested in the habit and who was not vested until two years later because she was too young. On the vigil of the feast the nuns came as usual and while they were there I had an inspiration. I thought within myself: "Tomorrow is the feast of our Blessed Mother. If I should promise her that if she would cure me I would become a Sister of Charity, what would happen?"

This thought consoled me. I told it to Sister Leonilda and she promised that if I were cured I could be vested with the novice of whom I spoke above. All that remained was that I should make the promise the next morning after Holy Communion. Monsignor came to hear my confession and he immediately gave his permission. He also gave me another consolation. We made a perpetual vow of virginity together that evening, a vow which previously he had never allowed me to make. He renewed it and I made it for the first and last time. What tremendous graces, but I have never corresponded with them!

That evening I was in perfect peace. Night came and I went to sleep. All of a sudden I saw my Protector standing before me at the foot of my bed. He said to me: "Gemma, make the vow to become a religious gladly, but add nothing else." "But why!" I asked. Touching me on the forehead while he looked at me and smiled, he answered: "My sister!" I did not understand what it was all about. To thank him, I kissed his habit. He took the woolen heart (which Passionists wear on their breast), had me kiss it and then placed it on the sheet over my heart and again said to me: "My sister!" With that he disappeared.

The next morning there was nothing on the sheet. I went to Communion and afterwards made my promise but added nothing else. I did not speak of this either with the nuns or with my confessor. At that time and many times later the nuns reminded me of my vow because they thought I had promised to become a Sister of Charity, and they told me that our Blessed Mother could cure me. Jesus graciously accepted my vow and my poor heart was very glad.

MIRACULOUS CURE (MARCH 3,1899)

But the months passed and I did not get any better. On the fourth of January the doctors tried another remedy. They cauterized me in 12 places along the spine. That was enough. I began to grow worse. Besides the usual pains, on January 28 I began to suffer an unbearable headache. The doctor whom they called said that it was very dangerous (calling it a tumor of the brain). They could not operate because I was suffering from extreme weakness. I grew worse from day to day and on the second of February they brought me Holy Viaticum. I made my confession and I was waiting to go and be with Jesus. It seemed that it would be soon. The doctors, thinking that I was no longer conscious, said among themselves that I would not live until midnight. Live Jesus!

One of my teachers in school (of whom I have spoken above)[26] came to see me and to tell me farewell saying that she would see me on heaven. But nonetheless she begged me to make a novena to Blessed Margaret Mary Alacoque, assuring me that she would gain for me the grace either of being cured perfectly, or else of entering heaven immediately after death.

This teacher, before she would leave my bed made me promise her to begin the novena that same evening. It was February 18. I did begin it. That very evening I said the prayers for the first time. The next day I forgot them. On the 20th I began all over again, but once more I forgot to say the prayers. This was very poor attention to prayer, was it not, dear Father?

On the 23rd I began for the third time (that is, I intended to), but a little before midnight I heard a rosary rattling and I felt a hand resting on my forehead. I heard someone begin saying the Pater, Ave and Gloria and repeating them nine times. I could hardly answer the prayers because my pain was so intense. Then that same voice that had said the prayers asked me: "Do you want to be cured?" "It's all the same to me," I answered. "Yes," he said, "you will be cured. Pray with faith to the Heart of Jesus. Every evening until the novena is finished I will be here with you and we will pray to the Heart of Jesus together." "And Blessed Margaret Mary?" I asked. "You may add three Gloria's in her honor."

The same thing happened for nine successive nights. The same person came every evening, placed his hand on my forehead and we recited together the prayers of the Sacred

---

[26] Sister Giulia Sestini of the Institute of St. Zita.

Heart, after which he had me add three Gloria's in honor of Bl. Margaret Mary.[27]

It was the second to last day of the novena and I wanted to receive communion on the last day which was the first Friday of March. I sent for my confessor and went to confession. The next morning I received communion. What happy moments I spent with Jesus! He kept repeating to me: "Gemma, do you want to be cured?" I was so moved that I could not answer. Poor Jesus! The grace had been given. I was cured.

TENDERNESS OF JESUS

"My daughter," Jesus said embracing me, "I give myself entirely to you and you will be entirely mine." I saw clearly that Jesus had taken my parents from me and sometimes this made me discouraged, because I believed myself abandoned. That morning I complained to Jesus about this and he, always so good and tender, said to me: "My daughter, I will always be with you. I will be your father and she (indicating our Mother of Sorrows) will be your mother. He who is my hands can never lack fatherly help. You will never lack anything even though I have taken away from you all earthly consolation and support. Come, draw near to me, you are my daughter. Are you not happy to be the daughter of Jesus and Mary?" The overwhelming affections to which Jesus gave rise in my heart kept me from answering.

After about two hours had passed I arose. Those in the house wept for joy. I too was happy, not because I was cured but because Jesus had chosen me to be his daughter. Before leaving me that morning Jesus said to me: "To the grace that

---

[27] From other sources we know that the person who appeared to her was St. Gabriel.

has been given you this morning there will be added many more and greater ones." And this has been so true because Jesus has always protected me in a special way. I have treated him only with coldness and indifference and in exchange he has given me only signs of infinite love.

HUNGER FOR THE EUCHARIST

From that time on I could hardly bear not to receive Jesus every morning. But I was not able to do so. I had the permission of my confessor to do so but I was so weak that I could hardly stand on my feet. On the second Friday of March 1899, I went to church for the first time to receive Holy Communion. And from then until now I have continued to go every day. I missed only now and then because my great sins made me unworthy, or as a chastisement imposed on me by my confessor.

WITH THE VISITANDINE SISTERS

That same morning, the second Friday of March, the Visitandine Sisters wanted to see me. I went to see them and they promised me that in May I could come to them and make a course of spiritual exercises. Furthermore, they told me that if my desire proved to be a true vocation they would take me into the convent in June for good. I felt great contentment in the thought of this, especially since Monsignor was in perfect accord with the idea.

PART VI

HOLY WEEK OF 1899

The month of March passed with me receiving communion every morning and Jesus was filling me with unspeakable consolations. Then came Holy Week.[28] I wanted so much to attend the sacred functions. But Jesus had arranged otherwise. During the Holy Week he asked of me a great sacrifice. Wednesday of Holy Week came (no sign had been given me except that when I received communion Jesus made himself felt in a most wonderful manner).

HER GUARDIAN ANGEL AS MASTER AND GUIDE

From the moment when I got up from my sick bed, my Guardian Angel began to be my master and guide. He corrected me every time I did something wrong and he taught me to speak but little and that only when I was spoken to. One day when those in the house were speaking of some person and were not speaking very well of her, I wanted to speak up but the angel gave me a severe rebuke. He taught me to keep my eyes cast down, and one time in church he

---

[28] Elsewhere, Gemma wrote a fuller account of this Holy Week. The account may be found in the Italian work: Estasi, Diario, Autobiografia, Scritti Vari di S. Gemma Galgani, p. 286ff.

reproved me strongly saying to me: "Is this the way to conduct yourself in the presence of God?" And another time he chided me in this way: "If you are not good I will not let you see me anymore." He taught me many times how to act in the presence of God; that is, to adore him in his infinite goodness, his infinite majesty, his mercy and in all his attributes.

FIRST HOLY HOUR—JESUS CRUCIFIED

As I said before, we were in Holy Week. It was Wednesday. My confessor had finally decided that it would be well for me to make a general confession as I had desired for so long a time. He chose a late hour on Wednesday for me to do this. In his infinite mercy Jesus gave me a very deep sorrow for my sins and here is how it came about. On Thursday evening I began to make the Holy Hour. (I had promised the Sacred Heart that if I were cured I would make the Holy Hour every Thursday without fail.) This was the first time I had made it out of bed. I had made it on the preceding Thursdays but in bed because my confessor would not let me make it any other way on account of my extreme weakness. But from the time of my general confession he permitted me to make it out of bed.

I began therefore, to make the Holy Hour[29] but I felt myself so full of sorrow for my sins that it was a time of continual martyrdom. However, in the midst of this sorrow there was one comfort, namely, weeping. This was both a comfort

---

[29] The practice of making the Holy Hour in union with the Agonizing Jesus had been suggested to her by Sister Giulia Sestina a few days before her miraculous cure. This nun had given her a prayer book containing a method of making the Holy Hour. An English translation of these same Holy Hour prayers appeared in THE SIGN, December 1926, Vol. 8, No. 5.

and a relief to me. I spent the entire hour praying and weeping. Finally, being very tired, I sat down but the sorrow continued. I became entirely recollected and after a little bit, all of a sudden, I felt my strength fail. (It was only with great difficulty that I was able to get up and lock the door to the room.) Where was I? Dear Father, I found myself before Jesus Crucified. He was bleeding all over. I lowered my eyes and the sight filled me with pain. I made the sign of the cross and immediately my anguish was succeeded by peace of soul.[30] I continued to feel an even stronger sorrow for my sins and I had not the courage to raise my eyes and look at Jesus. I prostrated myself on the floor and remained there for several hours. "My daughter," He said, "Behold these wounds. They have all been opened for your sins. But now, be consoled, for they have all been closed by your sorrow. Do not offend me anymore. Love me as I have always loved you. Love me." This he repeated several times.

The vision vanished and I returned to my senses. From that time on I began to have a great horror for sin (which was the greatest grace Jesus has given me). The wounds of Jesus remained so vividly impressed in my mind that they have never been effaced.

GOOD FRIDAY (MARCH 31,1899)

On the morning of Good Friday I received Holy Communion[31] and I would have liked to have gone to the services that

---

[30] Mystical writers give this as one of the criteria to judge whether an apparition is from God.

[31] She did not receive Communion from the hands of a priest, but miraculously, as is evident from her words in this paragraph. This was not the only time she received our Lord in this way. Father Germanus says: "This is known to have happened only three times. But there is reason to believe that it happened many more times."

day in honor of the Agony. But my family would not permit it even though I wept. With great difficulty I made this first sacrifice to Jesus. And Jesus, always so generous, saw fit to reward me even though I made the sacrifice with much difficulty. I shut myself in my room, therefore, to make the hour of Agony alone. But I was not alone. My Guardian Angel came to me and we prayed together. We assisted Jesus in all his sufferings and compassionated our Mother in her sorrows. But my angel did not fail to give me a gentle rebuke, telling me that I should not cry when I had to make a sacrifice to Jesus; but, that I should rather thank those who offered me the occasion to do so.

This was the first time and also the first Friday on which Jesus made himself felt so strongly in my soul. And although I did not receive communion from the hands of a priest because it was impossible, Jesus nevertheless came himself and communicated himself to me. And this union with him was so overwhelming that I remained as if stupefied.

Jesus spoke very strongly to me. "What are you doing?" he said to me. "What have you to say? Aren't you ever moved at all?" Then it was that, not being able to resist any longer, I blurted out: "Oh Jesus, how is it that you who are most perfect and all holy choose one so full of coldness and imperfection to love?" He answered: "I am burning with desire to unite myself with you. Hasten to receive me every morning. But remember that I am a father and a zealous spouse. Will you be my daughter and my faithful spouse?"

I made a thousand promises to Jesus that morning but, my God, how soon I forgot them! I always felt a horror for sin but at the same time I was always committing it. And Jesus was not satisfied with me though he ever consoled me, sending my Guardian Angel to be my guide in everything.

After these things happened to me I felt that I should speak to my confessor about them. I went to confession but I did not have the courage. I left the confessional without saying anything about it.[32] I returned home and on entering my room I noticed that my angel was weeping. I didn't have the courage to ask him what he was crying about but he himself told me. "Do you want to be deprived of seeing me anymore? You are a bad girl. You are hiding things from your confessor. Remember this, and I am telling you for the last time, if you ever hide anything else from your confessor I will never let you see me anymore. Never, never." I fell to my knees and he told me to make an act of contrition and made me promise to reveal everything to my confessor. With this he pardoned me in the name of Jesus.

A SEVERE REPROOF FROM JESUS

The month of April had arrived. I was impatiently awaiting the time when I could go to the Visitandine Sisters to make a retreat as they had promised me. One time, it was one morning after communion, Jesus told me about something that had displeased him very much. I had committed the fault the evening before.

Two young girls who were friends of one of my sisters used to come to our house and though their conversation was not bad, it was worldly. This time I took part in the conversation adding my little bit like the others. But the next morning Jesus rebuked me so severely that it inspired in me a great terror and I would have desired never to see or speak to anyone else.

Nevertheless, Jesus continued to make Himself felt in my soul every day, filling me with consolation. And I, on the

---

[32] Notice Gemma's great repugnance to manifesting the gifts of God: a clear indication of her profound humility.

other hand, continued to turn my back to him and offend him without any sorrow.

PART VII

THIRST FOR LOVE AND SUFFERING

Two sentiments were engendered in my heart after the first time Jesus made himself felt and allowed me to see him covered with blood. The first was to love him even to the point of sacrifice. But since I did not know how to love him truly, I asked my confessor to teach me and he answered as follows: "How do we learn to read and write? We practice reading and writing over and over until we finally learn how." This answer did not convince me. In fact, I didn't know what he meant. Often I asked him the same question, but he always gave me the same answer.

The other sentiment that sprung up in my heart after having seen Jesus was a desire to suffer something for him seeing that he had suffered so much for me. I got myself a thick rope which I took secretly from the well, made several knots in it and put it around my body. But I didn't have it on a quarter of an hour before my Guardian Angel reproved me and made me take it off because I had not asked my confessor's permission and obtained it. But my great affliction was not being able to love Jesus as I wished. I tried eagerly not to offend him but my bad inclination to evil was so strong that without a special grace of God I would have fallen into hell.

"LEARN HOW TO LOVE"

Not knowing how to love Jesus caused me much concern but he, in his infinite goodness, was never ashamed to humiliate me in order that he might become my Master. One evening when I was at prayer he came to bring peace to my soul. I felt myself entirely recollected and I found myself a second time before Jesus Crucified. He said to me: "Look daughter, and learn how to love," and he showed me his five open wounds. "Do you see this cross, these thorns, these nails, these bruises, these tears, these wounds, this blood? They are all works of love and of infinite love. Do you see how much I have loved you? Do you really want to love me? Then first learn to suffer. It is by suffering that one learns to love."

On seeing this I experienced a new sorrow and thinking of the infinite love of Jesus for us and the sufferings he had undergone for our salvation, I fell fainting to the floor and I remained thus for several hours. All that had happened to me during these times of prayer brought me such great consolation that although they were prolonged for several hours I was not tired out.

I continued to make the Holy Hour every Thursday, but sometimes it happened that it lasted until about two o'clock because I was with Jesus and almost always he gave me a share in the grief that he experienced in the garden at the sight of my many sins and those of the entire world. It was such a deep sorrow that it could well be compared to the agony of death. After all this I would experience so sweet a calm and consolation that I had to give vent to it in tears. And these tears made me taste an incomprehensible love and increased in me the desire to love Jesus and to suffer for him.

IN THE MONASTERY OF THE VISITANDINES

The time of the retreat I wanted so much was drawing near, and on the first of May, 1899 at three o'clock I went into the convent. I felt that I was entering heaven itself. What consolations! For the first time I forbade those of my family to come to see me during that time because those days were all for Jesus. On the evening that I entered, Monsignor came and granted me the permission (as the Mother Superior desired) that I should not make the retreat in private but that I should make it as a kind of test, that is, doing all that the nuns did. This consoled me in one way, but in another way it displeased me because that way I could not be as recollected. But I wanted to obey without a word. The Mother Superior put the Mistress of Novices in charge of me. She gave me a schedule to follow while I was there.

I had to rise at five o'clock, go to the choir at 5:30, receive Holy Communion and then recite Prime and Sext with the nuns. Then I would leave the choir to take breakfast and a half hour later go to my cell. At nine o'clock I would go to the choir again for the community Mass and to recite None. Then, at 9:30 Monsignor would come to give me a little conference if he could. But when he could not come I would make a meditation from a book that he sent me during that time and then he would come in the evening to give me a little talk. At 10:15 when the meditation was over I would make a visit to Jesus with the nuns. From 10:30 until 11:30 was the dinner hour and from then until 12:30 we had recreation (I had permission from Monsignor to spend only one recreation period a day with the nuns because I wanted to spend the evening recreation in the choir with Jesus). At 12:30 I went to the novitiate where there was work until three o'clock. At three we went again to the choir to recite

Vespers and then the community gathered for an instruction from the superior until five o'clock. At five we went again to the choir to recite Compline which was followed by an hour of meditation which we made in any manner we pleased. After meditation we went to the refectory again and then to recreation. This recreation period I spent with the superior in her room or else in the choir. At 8:30 the community gathered again for about a half hour and at 9:00 we recited Matins and went to bed.

Dear Father, it seemed to me that this type of life was almost too easy for the nuns, and rather than becoming attached to it I began instead to dislike that manner of life. The novices, who all had special concern for me, would advise me now and then and speak of those things which were more appealing about the community, but I gave no thought to these things. The thing that afflicted me was the thought that I had to return to the world. I would have preferred to remain there (even though that form of life did not appeal to me) than return again to those places where there were many occasions of offending Jesus. I begged Monsignor to grant me the permission to remain at the convent.

With the permission of the Mother Superior and the entire community, I asked permission of the Archbishop[33] to remain there, but he would not grant it, saying that my health was still so poor that I was wearing an iron brace on my back to hold it straight (I haven't the slightest idea who told the Archbishop). The Mother Superior commanded me under obedience, therefore, to take off the brace. I wept on receiving this command because I well knew that I could not do without it. I ran to the novitiate and prayed to my dear Child Jesus. Then I hastened to my room. I took it off, and

---

[33] Msgr. Nicola Ghilardo, archbishop of Lucca. Msgr. Volpi was his Auxiliary at this time.

though nearly two years have passed since then, I have never worn it again and I am doing very well.

The superior, on hearing of this, hastened to tell the Monsignor that he might inform the Archbishop. There was only one more day left of the retreat and Monsignor came to hear my confession. He asked me if I would remain in the convent for twelve more days because on May 21 some of the Sisters were going to make their profession and they wanted me to be present.

I was infinitely happy to remain with them but I was convinced of one thing: that life was too easy for me. I had sinned so much that I must do penance. I revealed my fears to Jesus after Communion and Jesus, ever considering my misery, consoled me and made himself felt in my soul, quieting me with consoling words. I was present, as Monsignor wished, at the profession of four novices. That morning I wept very much. Jesus was closer to me than usual and some of the Sisters who saw me came up to me and asked if I needed anything because I was at the point of losing my senses. (It was true. The nuns had forgotten to give me breakfast and they hadn't given me my dinner yet, so that I ate only after one o'clock).

But I received a stiff rebuke for this as I deserved. I should have gone to the refectory on my own when the bell rang.[34] But I was ashamed or rather, (listen, dear Father to what limit my malice, or rather my human respect leads me) the Mother Superior always kept me beside her wherever we were. But that day of Profession the newly professed nuns took their place alongside the superior so that I remained outside without eating. My pride would not allow me to take second place to them.

---

[34] Notice how Gemma takes pains to accuse herself.

My God, I merited worse, but Jesus still supported me. He chastised me by not making himself felt for several days. I wept much on account of this but Jesus sent my Guardian Angel to me again and he said to me: "Happy you, daughter, who deserve such a just punishment." I understood none of these words but they brought consolation to my heart.

RETURNS TO HER FAMILY

NOSTALGIA FOR THE CLOISTER—DELUDED HOPES

My God! There came another sorrow. The next day I had to leave the convent and return home. I wanted that day never to come, but it was at hand. At five o'clock in the afternoon on May 21, 1899, I had to leave. In tears, I asked the blessing of the Mother Superior, said good—bye to the nuns, and left. My God! What grief!

But an even greater sorrow was to follow soon on this one. I returned to my family but I was no longer able to adapt myself. My mind and heart were fixed on the idea of becoming a religious and no one could discourage me from it. In order to leave the world I seriously considered becoming a Visitandine Nun at once. Almost every day I would hasten to the monastery and the sisters promised me that in the month of June, on the feast of the Sacred Heart, they would accept me.

I must say, however, that my heart was not fully at rest because I knew that the Visitandine life was too easy for me. And many times, on different occasions, Jesus said to me in my heart: "Daughter, you need a more austere rule." But I very seldom paid any attention to these words and I remained firm in resolution.

We began the month of June and I noticed that the nuns were changing their attitude. Every time I went to see the Superior they told me that she could not come and she would send first one then another to talk to me. They began to speak seriously to me, telling me that unless I could bring at least four medical certificates with me I would not be accepted. I tried to fulfill this requirement but all efforts were in vain. The doctors would not cooperate and one day the nuns told me that when I brought the certificates they would receive me immediately, but until then absolutely not. This decision did not disturb me in the least because Jesus was consoling me with so many graces.

A VERY PRECIOUS GRACE—THE STIGMATA

On the 8th of June[35] after communion Jesus told me that that evening he would give me a very great grace. I went that same day to confession and I told Monsignor about it. He told me to be very attentive so that I could tell him all about it afterwards.

Evening came and all of a sudden, earlier than usual, I felt an interior sorrow for my sins far deeper than I had ever experienced before. In fact, it brought me very, very close to death. After this, all the powers of my soul became recollected. My intellect could think of nothing but my sins and the offense they gave to God. My memory recalled all my sins to mind and made me see all the torments that Jesus had suffered in order to save me. And my will made me detest them and promise to be willing to suffer anything in order to expiate them. My mind was flooded with thoughts, thoughts of sorrow, of love, of fear, of hope and of comfort.

Following on this interior recollection I was quickly rapt out of my senses and I found myself before my heavenly Mother. At her right stood my Guardian Angel who told me

---

[35] Thursday, June 8, 1899, octave of Corpus Christi and vigil of the Feast of the Sacred Heart.

to make an act of contrition. When I had finished it my blessed Mother said to me: "Daughter, in the name of Jesus all your sins are forgiven." Then she added: "Jesus my Son loves you very much and he wants to give you a grace. Do you know how to make yourself worthy of it?" In my misery I did not know what to answer. She continued: "I will be your Mother. Will you be a true daughter?" She spread her mantle and covered me with it.

At that moment Jesus appeared with all his wounds open. But blood no longer came out of those wounds. Rather, flames as of fire issued forth from them and in a moment those flames came to touch my hands, feet and heart. I felt as if I would die. I fell to the floor. But my Mother supported me keeping me covered with her mantle. I had to remain for several hours in that position. Then the Blessed Mother kissed me on the forehead, and it all disappeared and I found myself kneeling on the floor. But I still felt an intense pain in my hands, feet and heart.

I arose to lie down on the bed and I noticed that blood was flowing from those places where I felt pain. I covered these parts as best I could and then, with the help of my angel, I was able to get in bed. These sufferings and pains, although they afflicted me, filled me with perfect peace. The next morning I was able to go to communion only with great difficulty and I put on a pair of gloves in order to hide my hands. I could hardly stand on my feet and I thought I would die any minute. The sufferings continued until three o'clock Friday afternoon, the solemn feast of the Sacred Heart of Jesus.[36] I should have told these things to my confessor at once but instead I went to confession several times without

---

[36] This reception of the stigmata took place at the home of Gemma, 13 Via del Briscione. This street is now called Via S. Gemma Galgani.

saying anything about them. He asked me about it several times but I would not tell him.

PART VIII

THE STIGMATA IS REPEATED

Meanwhile, some time passed and every Thursday about eight o'clock I began to feel the usual sufferings. And every time this happened to me I first felt a deep and intense sorrow for my sins. This caused me more suffering than the pains in my hands, feet, head and heart. This sorrow for my sins reduced me to a state of grief close to death. But in spite of this wonderful grace from God I did not improve but rather I committed numerous sins every day. I was disobedient and insincere with my confessor, always hiding something or other from him. My angel admonished me many times, telling me that if I continued to do this he would not allow me to see him anymore. But I did not obey him and he did go away, or rather, he would only hide himself for a while.

ARDENT DESIRE FOR THE CLOISTER
JESUS COMFORTS AND REPROVES HER

During this time my desire to become a nun kept increasing. I told my confessor about this but he gave me little consolation. I spoke to Jesus about it and one morning when I felt this desire more strongly than usual Jesus said to me:

"Daughter, what are you afraid of? Hide this desire in my heart and no one will be able to take it away." Jesus spoke to me in this way because, since this desire to go to the convent and unite myself forever with Jesus was so great, I feared someone would be able to take it away from me. But Jesus immediately consoled me with these words and others that I have forgotten.

Jesus never failed to make himself felt and seen, especially when I was afflicted. One day (which deserves special mention) I had been scolded, as I always deserved, by one of my brothers because I was going out for a while to pray in the church. During the little dispute that we had I suffered a slight blow, which I deserved, and I was complaining about it. Jesus was not at all pleased and he reproved me with certain words which truly hurt me. He said: "Daughter, are you also adding your share to the pain of my Heart? I have exalted you to be my daughter and honored you with the title of my servant, and now how do you behave? You are an arrogant daughter, and unfaithful servant. You are bad!" These words made such an impression on my heart that even though Jesus added new crosses after that, he always gave me the strength to thank him, and not to complain anymore. Jesus gave me an even stronger rebuke one time in these words, which at that time I did not understand but I later found them to be true. He said: "Daughter, you complain too much in adversity, you are too perplexed in temptation and too timid to control your affections. I give you nothing but love: love in adversity, in prayer, in affronts, love in everything. And tell me, daughter, can you deny me such a just satisfaction and such a little recompense?" I could not find words to answer Jesus. My heart almost burst with sorrow, and I said the following words which I remember so well: "My heart, O Jesus, is ready to do everything. It is ready to burst with sorrow if you will it, my God!"

MISSION AT ST. MARTIN

The month of June was almost over and near the end of the month a mission began in the church of St. Martin. I always preferred to miss the mission rather than miss the sermons on the Sacred Heart at the Visitation church. But finally the latter ended and I began to go to hear the mission sermons in St. Martin Church.[37] I cannot describe the impression made on me when I saw those priests preach! The impression was very great because I saw that they were clothed with the same kind of habit that Brother Gabriel was wearing the first time I saw him. I was seized with such an affection for them that I never missed a sermon from that day until the end of the mission.

The last day of the mission arrived and all the people were gathered in the church for the general Communion. I was among the large crowd and Jesus, who was greatly pleased, made Himself strongly felt by my soul and he said to me: "Gemma, do you like the habit that priest is wearing?" (He indicated a Passionist who was somewhat distant from me.) I did not answer with words but my heart answered him with its palpitations. He added: "Would you like to be clothed with the same habit?" "My God!" I exclaimed, "Yes." Jesus continued, "you will be a daughter of my Passion, and a well beloved daughter. One of these sons (of the Passion) will be your father. Go and reveal everything." And I saw that Jesus indicated Father Ignatius.

I obeyed. On the last day of the mission I went to church but no matter how hard I tried I could hardly bring myself to

---

[37] This mission was held in the metropolitan Church of St. Martin from June 25 to July 9, 1899. It was preached by the following Passionist Fathers: Cajetan, Adalbert, Callistus and Ignatius.

speak of the affairs of my soul. Instead of going to Father Ignatius I went to Father Cajetan and with great difficulty I told him about all that had happened to me as I have here related. He listened to me with infinite patience and he promised he would return to Lucca the following Monday and then he would have more time for my confession. Such was the arrangement. A week later I was able to go to confession to him again and I continued to go to him the next few times. At this time, and by means of this priest, I made the acquaintance of a lady to whom I have to this day the love of a mother and whom I have always regarded as such.[38]

THE THREE VOWS

The only reason I went to confession to this priest was this: my ordinary confessor had forbidden me many times to make the three vows of chastity, obedience and poverty because it would be impossible to observe them as long as I remained in the world. I, who had always had a great desire to make them, made use of that occasion and this was the first thing I asked of him. He immediately gave me the permission to make them from the 5th of July to the solemn feast of the 8th of September and then they were to be renewed. I was very happy at this and it became one of my greatest consolations. At the cost of great patience on the part of this priest and with great shame on my part I revealed everything to him. I told him of all the particular graces the Lord had given me, the visits from my Guardian Angel, the presence of Jesus and also some penances which of my own accord and without any permission I had been performing every day. He at once commanded me to cease doing these

---

[38] This lady was Cecilia Giannini with whom Gemma lived during the last years of her life.

things and he took from me some of the instruments of penance that I had been using. Then this priest spoke clearly to me and told me that he was not in a position to direct me properly and that I must reveal everything to my confessor. I was in no way minded to follow this advice because I foresaw a great struggle and I feared the danger of being abandoned by Monsignor on account of my lack of sincerity and confidence in him. On no condition would I tell this priest the name of my confessor. I told him that I did not know who he was and I might have even invented a false name. I don't remember. But my little trick did not go far. To my great shame, I was discovered. Father Cajetan knew that Monsignor was my confessor but he could not speak to him about me unless I gave him permission. Finally, after keeping him in suspense for a while I gave him permission and it turned out that the two of them were in complete agreement. Monsignor gave me permission to go to this Father to confession whenever I wished and did not scold me as I had indeed deserved. I told Monsignor about the vows I had made and he approved of them adding to them a fourth vow, namely, sincerity with my confessor. He further commanded me to remain hidden and to speak of the affairs of my soul to no one but himself.

FUTILE VISIT BY THE DOCTOR REPROOFS FROM JESUS

Meanwhile the Friday occurrences continued and Monsignor thought it well to have a doctor visit me during one of them without my knowing it. But Jesus warned me saying: "Tell your confessor that in the presence of the doctor I will do none of the things that he desires." Following the advice of Jesus I told my confessor about this but he did as he had planned, and events turned out as Jesus had said, as you already know. Dear Father, from that day a new life began for me and I could tell you many things here, but, Jesus willing, I will tell them to you when we are alone (in the confessional). This was the first and best humiliation that Jesus gave me. Nevertheless, my great pride and selflove resented it. But Jesus in his infinite charity continued to give me his graces and favors. One day Jesus lovingly said to me (dear Father, because Jesus spoke these words to me I will tell them to you alone, but maybe you will understand them without me explaining them): "Daughter, what can I say when you, in all your doubts, afflictions and adversities think always of yourself instead of me. When you always hasten to find some relief and comfort rather than turn to me?"

Dear Father, do you understand? This was a just rebuke from Jesus, one that I knew I well deserved. But nonetheless I continued as usual and Jesus again reproved me saying: "Gemma, do you think that I am not offended when in your great needs you turn to things that cannot bring you consolation instead of turning to me? I suffer, daughter, when I see you forget me." This last reproof was enough for me and it succeeded in detaching me entirely from every creature in order to seek my Creator in everything.[39]

FATHER GERMANUS

I received another prohibition from my Confessor regarding the extraordinary experiences on Thursdays and Fridays, and Jesus obeyed for a little while. But then they returned as formerly and even more so. I was no longer afraid to reveal everything (to my confessor) and he told me emphatically that if he was not allowed to see these things clearly he would

---

[39] Father Germanus, to whom Gemma wrote her first letter on January 29, 1900, came to Lucca in early September of the same year.

not believe in such fantasies. Without losing any time, that very day I said a special prayer to Jesus in the Blessed Sacrament for this intention. And behold! As often happened to me, I felt myself become interiorly recollected and soon I was rapt out of my senses.

I found myself before Jesus but he was not alone. Standing beside him was a man with white hair and from his habit I knew that he was a Passionist. He had his hands joined and he was praying, praying fervently. As I looked at him Jesus said to me: "Daughter, do you know him?" I told him "No," as was true. "Look," he added, "that priest will be your director and it will be he who will recognize in you, miserable creature, the infinite work of my mercy."

After this happened I thought no more of it. But one day I chanced to see a little portrait. It was without a doubt a picture of the priest that I had seen beside Jesus though the likeness was very poor. Dear Father, my intimate union with you in prayer began from the moment when I first saw you with Jesus in my vision. From then on I always wanted to have you with me but the more I desired it, the more it seemed impossible. From that day on I would pray many times a day for this and after several months Jesus consoled me by having you come to see me.[40] Now I will say no more because from that time until now you have always known me and you know everything.

---

[40] It is not clear why Gemma wrote these two letters. In the manuscript they are a little obscure.

CATHOLIC WAY PUBLISHING

QUALITY PAPERBACKS AND E-BOOKS

True Devotion to Mary: With Preparation for Total Consecration
by Saint Louis de Montfort
    6" x 9" Hardback:..ISBN–13: 978-1-78379-004-3
    6" x 9" Paperback:..ISBN–13: 978-1-78379-011-1
    5" x 8" Paperback:..ISBN–13: 978-1-78379-000-5
    MOBI E-Book:..ISBN–13: 978-1-78379-001-2
    EPUB E-Book: ISBN–13: 978-1-78379-002-9

The Secret of the Rosary by Saint Louis de Montfort
    5" x 8" Paperback:..ISBN–13: 978-1-78379-310-5
    MOBI E-Book:..ISBN–13: 978-1-78379-311-2
    EPUB E-Book: ISBN–13: 978-1-78379-312-9

The Imitation of Christ by Thomas a Kempis
    5" x 8" Paperback:..ISBN–13: 978-1-78379-037-1
    MOBI E-Book:..ISBN–13: 978-1-78379-038-8
    EPUB E-Book: ISBN–13: 978-1-78379-039-5

My Daily Prayers by Catholic Way Publishing
    5" x 8" Paperback:..ISBN–13: 978-1-78379-027-2
    MOBI E-Book:..ISBN–13: 978-1-78379-028-9
    EPUB E-Book: ISBN–13: 978-1-78379-029-6

The Mystical City of God: Popular Abridgement
by Venerable Mary of Agreda
    5" x 8" Paperback:..ISBN–13: 978-1-78379-063-0
    MOBI E-Book:..ISBN–13: 978-1-78379-064-7
    EPUB E-Book: ISBN–13: 978-1-78379-065-4

The Three Ages of the Interior Life: Prelude of Eternal Life
by Reverend Reginald Garrigou-Lagrange O.P.
    6" x 9" Paperback Volume 1:............................ISBN–13: 978-1-78379-378-5
    6" x 9" Paperback Volume 2:............................ISBN–13: 978-1-78379-379-2
    MOBI E-Book:..ISBN–13: 978-1-78379-376-1
    EPUB E-Book: ISBN–13: 978-1-78379-377-8

www.catholicwaypublishing.com
London, England, UK
2013

Made in the USA
Columbia, SC
21 November 2017